THE FANG F

Fright at the Fair

Denmark House, ...
Camberwell, SE5 8SN

Written by Sheryl Webster

Illustrated by Pete Williamson

The Fang Family

Veino

Grandpa Fang

Mother Fang

Baby Fang

Small Fang

Father Fang

Did you know?

Vampires …

- have no reflection in a mirror.
- can change shape from human to bat.
- have sharp fangs.
- are afraid of sunlight.
- absolutely *hate* garlic.
- absolutely *love* to suck blood from people's necks. Mmmm, delicious!

Funny Fang Family Fact:

Mother Fang spends ages choosing what to wear, even though all her dresses are black and look the same!

Birthday Treat

It was Mother Fang's birthday
and Father Fang had planned a
treat. They were going to the fair!
However, so far things were not
going to plan.

Veino, their pet bloodhound, had
made a mess on the floor.

Baby Fang would
not have her nap because
she was afraid of the light.

Mother Fang could not decide
what to wear.

Just then, Small Fang came racing in through the door.

"Daaaaaad, I've got fang ache!"

"Oh no, that's all I need," sighed Father Fang. "No sweet treats for you tonight. Here's a small blood clot for the pain."

Grandpa Fang arrived home looking a little tatty. He had been out exercising his bat wings. "Oh, my eyes aren't what they used to be," he moaned.

Batty Behaviour

Finally, everyone was ready and the Fang Family flew off to the fair.

"Are we nearly there yet?" asked Small Fang.

"Soon!" smiled Father Fang.

"Are we nearly there *now*?"
asked Small Fang twenty seconds
later. Father Fang gritted his teeth.
Sometimes Small Fang could be
a real pain in the neck. Suddenly,
they noticed that Grandpa Fang
had vanished.

"Hang on," shouted Father Fang.

Father Fang found Grandpa
trying to bite a scarecrow.

"Oh dear!" he groaned. "How
many times must we tell you about
scarecrows?" He was getting fed up
with Grandpa's batty behaviour.

"But they just look so tasty!"
gabbled Grandpa Fang, as he spat
out a mouthful of sawdust.

Off they went again, but they soon got lost. "Let's ask that man for directions," suggested Mother Fang.

Father Fang flashed his best smile. "Very pleased to eat ... I mean meet you," he said. "Could you tell me the way to the Bleak Hill Fair?"

The man pointed and shot off.
"Wow! I never knew anybody
could jog that fast!" said Small Fang.

Fun and a Fright

Soon the Fangs heard the sound of a merry-go-round and the smell of fairground food.

"Can we eat now?" said Small Fang. He licked his lips as the other people walked by.

"No, we'll go on some rides first," said Mother Fang. "And remember, no sweet food for you until that fang ache is better."

Mother Fang chose the first ride because it was her birthday. She chose the ghost train.

"This just reminds me of home," Grandpa sniffed.

Small Fang gasped. "Wow, Mum! Can I decorate my room like this?"

Mother Fang gave Father Fang a juicy kiss. "This is so lovely, you old romantic, you!"

Next they headed for the Fun House. As they walked through the Hall of Mirrors, they stared at the stretched and squashed faces of the other people.

"Ooohhh, don't they look just so delicious!" said Mother Fang, smacking her lips hungrily. "I think we will have to eat soon."

"Let's hang around on the roller coaster for a while," said Father Fang. Screams of terror filled the air.

"Some people are such scaredy cats!" sniggered Small Fang. "Fancy being scared of a silly old roller coaster ride."

Suddenly Father Fang sniffed.
He looked in horror at the sign
below him.

He could hardly bear to read it ...

Lyndhurst Primary School
Denmark House, Grove Lane
Camberwell, SE5 8SN

Tasty corn on the cob
Delicious baked potatoes
Yummy burgers
Perfect pizzas
served with a variety
of fillings and
toppings including:
cheese, onions,
peppers and ga

... GARLIC!

Tasty corn on the cob
Delicious baked potatoes
Yummy burgers
Perfect pizzas
served with a variety
of fillings and
toppings including:
cheese, onions,
peppers and garlic

A Terrible Tizzy

Baby Fang began to blub. Small Fang started to cough. Mother Fang spluttered. Grandpa Fang clutched at his throat.

"Oh no!" said Father Fang. "Let's get out of here!"

But Grandpa Fang was in a
terrible tizzy. The smell had made
him so dizzy that he tossed and
tumbled. He knocked Father Fang
one way into the candy floss spinner,
and Mother Fang the other way into
the popcorn machine.

Luckily, when Father Fang was handed out on a stick, he managed to escape. But poor Mother Fang had to **POP** herself out of the popcorn box.

Then Father Fang
grabbed Grandpa.

Mother Fang
clutched Small Fang.

Small Fang
held on tight to
Baby Fang ...

and they all zoomed off home.

5

Fang Feast

Father Fang felt bad – Mother Fang's birthday treat was spoiled! Then he had an idea.

He telephoned Dial-a-Pizza.
"And NO GARLIC!" he said.

Grandpa whipped up some of his best ice-scream, and Small Fang and Baby Fang put up fresh cobwebs. Even the weather had changed for the better.

"This is the best birthday ever," said Mother Fang.